Surviving

the

FOOD

Desert

FROM THE DESK OF CHEF AMBER WILLIAMS

Surviving
the
FOOD
Desert

A collection of Recipes & Resources to help you survive & thrive in desolate places...and eat good along the journey.

ISBN: 979-8-218-24267-1

Printed in the United States, by IngramSpark

First Edition

Chef/Recipe Creation: Amber Williams
Creative Director: Morganne Stewart
Principal Photographer: Jackie Loubriel
Styling: Tamra Nicole, Tamra Nicole Styling Agency
Back Cover Photographer: Kianna Pierce, Pippy's Pix Media

This book is firstly dedicated to my Mom –

I'm sure you're aware you raised a wildly inquisitive and ambitious child, yet one who was rather observant as well. What you didn't know is,…. while I was observing you sift through boxes of random canned goods and food to create extraordinary meals, you were teaching me Agility & Creativity; while I complained about several nights of canned green peas and carrots, you were teaching me about Contentment; and as I silently observed you work, provide and thrive day-in and day-out, you were teaching me the power of Resilience, inadvertently training me for the life I live today.

This book is dedicated to YOU –

Every hidden survivor, silently fighting to overcome every obstacle, live abundantly despite lack, be seen when you're often not sought after or simply 'Make something out of nothing!" You may not have all you want, but everything you need is right within your reach - live to fight another day. Someone needs to observe how you survive, so they can thrive.

Desert
(des·ert | \ ˈde-zərt) n.

Arid [excessively dry] land with usually sparse vegetation; a desolate or forbidding area; FORSAKEN (Merriam Webster)

Food Desert

A food desert is an area that has limited access to affordable and nutritious food, in contrast with an area with higher access to supermarkets or vegetable shops with fresh foods, which is called a food oasis (Wikipedia).

Table of Contents

FOREWORD

Written by Cimajie Best

"Why should there be hunger and deprivation in any land, in any city, at any table, when man has the resources and the scientific know-how to provide all mankind with the basic necessities of life? There is no deficit in human resources. The deficit is in human will..."

Dr. Martin Luther King Jr.,
Where Do We Go From Here: Chaos or Community, 1967

What would Dr. King think if he knew that over 50 years later more than 34 million people, including 9 million children, in the United States are food insecure? What would he say if he knew that discriminatory practices, racial prejudice and barriers to education and employment have created a world where Black and Brown children are 3 times more likely to experience food insecurity than their counterparts? Would he be surprised, or would he readily identify with our current condition as the plight of the impoverished?

When Chef Amber asked if I would pen the foreword for this revolutionary work, I was both honored and stumped. How do I concisely introduce a work that is the answer to a problem that spans generations and geographies? What do you say to acquaint the reader with the man-made catastrophes that are food deserts?

After attempting to wax poetic to no avail, I decided that maybe the best place to start writing this forward is the beginning.

Chef Amber and I are from a neighborhood in Dallas called South Oak Cliff. While Oak Cliff is known for its historic homes, wide streets, and looming oak trees it's also known for having some of the lowest life expectancy rates in the county, the highest number of incarcerated residents of any zip code in the state, and a poverty rate almost twice that of the rest of the city.

These social determinants of health contribute significantly to health disparities and inequities.

If you grew up in a neighborhood like ours, a food desert, where people don't have access to grocery stores with fresh healthy foods, you are less likely to have adequate nutrition. Without proper nutrition you carry a higher risk of heart disease, diabetes, and obesity, as well as a shorter life expectancy. Imagine being a citizen of one of the wealthiest most influential countries in the world yet suffering from malnutrition.

Unfortunately, this story isn't unique to our neighborhood. There are food deserts in every state in America. Across this country individuals are making a choice between buying food and paying rent, between paying a doctor bill and feeding their children. Many households find that they "make too much money" to qualify for federal nutrition assistance but not enough to feed their families, thus they are turning to food banks for support.

This problem is real.

This problem is relentless.

Most of all, this problem is repairable, rectifiable, resolvable.

But not without you.

I encourage you to evaluate the food crisis in your own community. Engage with your local food bank and ask how you can support their efforts. Engage with your local nonprofits and plant community gardens. Engage with your local civic leaders and inquire about their plans to eradicate food insecurity in your community.

Remember there is no deficit in human resources, only human will.

And to those of us who call food deserts home. The ones of us who know what it's like to grocery shop at a convenience store or drive 15 minutes for fresh fruit. To the ones of us who make miracles out of the miniscule. This book is for you.

Let it inspire you to cook with care.

Let it inspire you to create desserts in the middle of a desert.

Let it inspire you to thrive in spite of.

Let it inspire you.

Cimajie Best

– Author & Cultural Agenda Setter

Introduction

I was raised in a food desert, grew up in a food desert; all to become an adult and still live in a food desert! "Why" you ask? Because I learned how to survive in a food desert.

For me, change doesn't happen when you alter your surroundings, change occurs when you shift your mindset. It's all in how you see your current circumstances, how you see yourself. The tools and actions you choose to put into practice when you're in survival mode are crucial.

Now I know you're probably thinking, "I thought this was a cookbook... where are the recipes and measurements?" But stick with me here. For me, food is more than a substance, it's a resource, a tool and a tangible aid for life lessons to be gleaned from. So, I don't want to just give you recipes you try once, to only then collect dust in your kitchen. For those who find themselves in their own "desert", whether physically, mentally or emotionally, I want to help you measure and shift your mindset while giving you ingredients to help you "make something out of nothing" - the real recipe to surviving your "desert". Much like a real desert, food deserts or food insecure communities are often seen as dry land, a land suffering from a drought, lack of resources, accessibility to "real" food, or as Merriam Webster would state "*forsaken*".

If you look at a map showing food disparaged communities in the Dallas/ Fort Worth area, one could almost say these areas of drought are almost in isolated zip codes, on an island of their own. However, the only difference I see, is when you're stranded on an island, the help normally comes to you - however this is not the reality for these forsaken communities in major cities all over the country. Instead, city officials and local government must lay a *red carpet* out over the barren land to, seemingly convince big name grocery store brands to even consider planting fruitful seeds in the communities that need them most - pretty ironic right?

But what happens when you can't make it 20 miles north to your closest fresh food mecca – rows of bountiful stores nestled so close together you'd think it was planned that way, sort of like the fast-food joints and countless fried chicken spots are abundantly planted in "other" communities. However, all hope is not lost, there is a silver lining on this path we're taking.

Like a rose sprouting from the concrete, noble citizens and organizations have started to create alternative ways to bring life back into the places others deemed unworthy. This movement has birthed countless community Garden initiatives, food share programs, and nonprofits who have banned together to tackle this growing epidemic. During the outbreak of Covid 19, I witnessed communities overflowing with numerous resources, like food pantries giving away an abundance of food daily, shared community food lockers where patrons can drop off food at any time for those in need to take freely, as well as the creation of several community gardens, probably my favorite part of what's come out of these survival tactics. Gardening projects teach kids and adults about growing their own sustainable food. People of all ethnicities working side by side to harvest abundance from the earth and bonding over the joy of sewing new life and joy into the places that desperately thirst for it.

As a chef from a food insecure area, one of my core values is sharing integral food education in food disparaged communities. I've come across individuals who have never seen a green bean outside of a can, never seen or heard of a spaghetti squash - more or less knew how to cook it. On behalf of the American Heart Association (AHA), I've helped teach classes on how to recreate dishes in a healthier fashion without sacrificing the flavor. I've seen blood sugar and cholesterol numbers drop, I've seen faces glow when their eyes were opened to new possibilities, and I've seen mindsets change. And this is why I want to help others survive their food desert.

As of 2022

1 in 6 Americans

are Food Insecure and struggle to eat *Daily*

Food Insecure refers to USDA's measure of lack of access to enough food for a healthy life for all household members uncertain availability of nutritional foods.

Here's how you Survive the *Food* Desert...

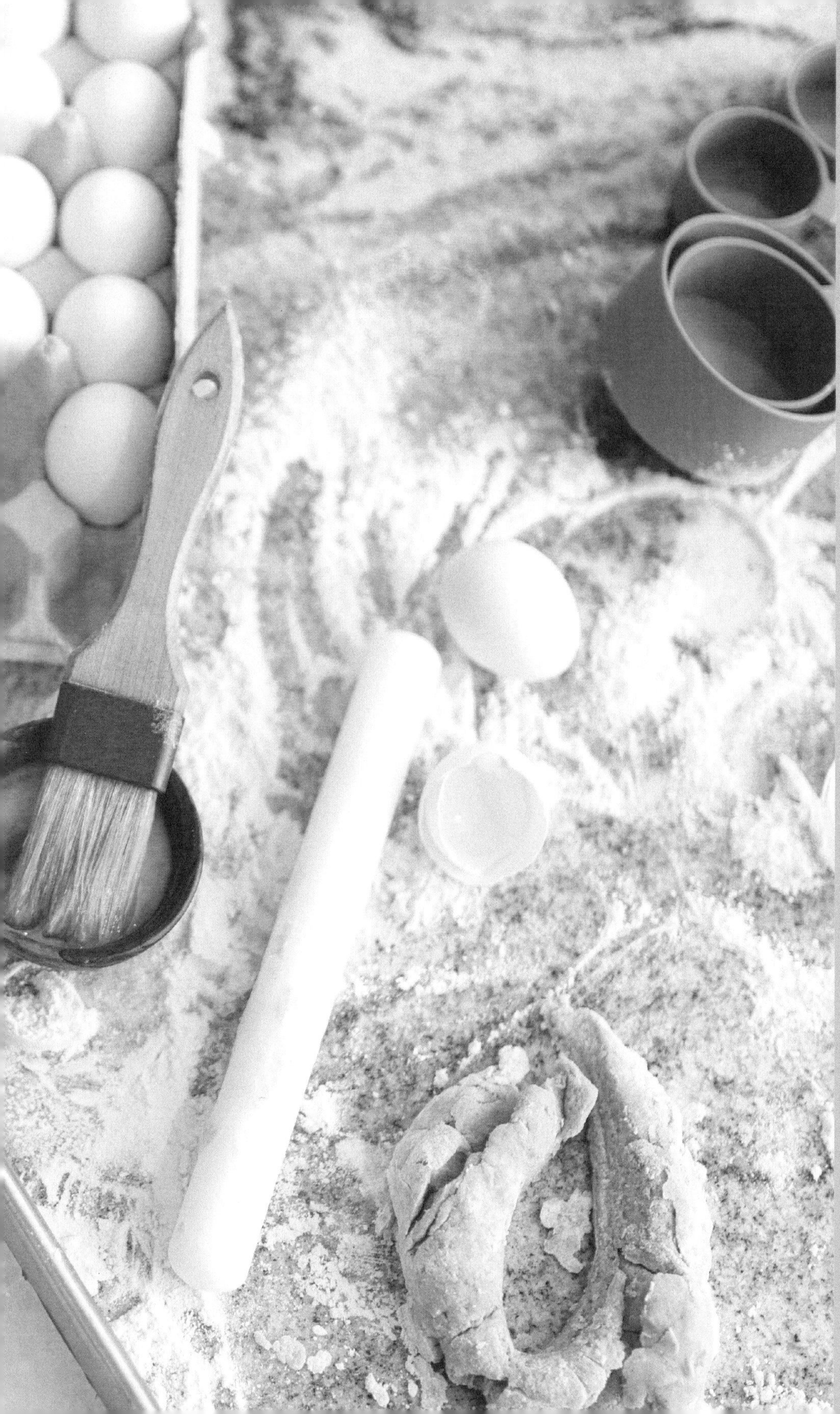

DAY STARTERS

Chapter 1

STAY GROUNDED

Root Yourself in Peace

While treading through a treacherous "desert season", your mental, emotional and spiritual **peace** should be at the top of your priority list. *Rooting* yourself in something that is immovable, dependable and solid creates certainty that no matter how the winds may blow, you have a foundation that can withstand the test of time and trials.

Enjoy these **Day Starters** as a fresh, unique way to get your morning started off right and ground yourself in Joy before you experience life for the day!

Cinna-butter Drop Biscuits

Serves: 12 | Prep Time: 10 minutes | Cook Time 12 minutes

2 cups AP Flour

1 tbsp. Baking Powder

1/2 tsp Salt

¼ cup Sugar

1/2 tsp Cinnamon

1 stick cold, cubed Butter

2 tbsp Shortening

1 cup Milk

1 Egg + 1 tbsp of water
  (for Egg Wash

Honey Butter:

3 tbsp room temp. Butter

1/2 tbsp Honey

1/4 tsp Ground cinnamon

Garlic Herb Cheddar Bay:

*Replace your cinnamon
  & sugar with:*

1 cup Shredded Cheddar

1 tsp Garlic Powder

1 tbsp Italian Seasoning

1. Preheat your oven to 375°F and prepare a baking sheet with parchment paper to create a non-stick surface.

2. In a large bowl, add your flour, baking powder, salt, sugar and cinnamon, then mix to combine.

3. Add your cubed butter and shortening and coat in the dry mix. With a fork or fingers, evenly distribute and break down the butter throughout your dry mixture. *Don't be afraid to use your hands and get dirty. This part is great for children to participate in.*

4. After your butter and shortening are broken into little buttery pellets, slowly stream in your milk and mix the dough with your hand or spoon. Be sure the wet and dry ingredients are well incorporated. *This process can also be done in a food processor in half the time.*

For Drop Biscuits: Drop large dollops of the biscuit dough onto your baking sheet, leaving space between each one for rising.

For Traditional Round Biscuits: Toss your dough onto a floured surface, pat or roll to your desired thickness, cut biscuit rounds with a cookie cutter or glass with a floured rim.

5. Brush those beautiful biscuits with your egg wash (1 beaten egg + tbsp of water) to create a golden brown color.

6. Bake for 12-15 minutes or until your biscuits are *bold, beautiful & brown.*

Baked Sweet Potato
with Apple & Onion Compote

Serves: 2-4 | Prep Time: 10 minutes | Cook Time: 50 minutes

2 Sweet potatoes

1 Apple (Fuji, Gala, etc.), sliced

1/2 Red onion, sliced

3/4 tsp Ground or Fresh Ginger

2 tsp Ground Cinnamon

1/4 tsp Ground Turmeric

1/4 tsp Ground Nutmeg

1/4 cup Brown Sugar

1/4 cup Raisins

1/2 cup store bought Granola

2 tbsp Butter

1 tbsp oil (Canola, grapeseed or avocado will work just fine)

1. With your oven set to 425°F, wash your sweet potatoes then poke the potatoes all over with a fork to allow steam to escape during the baking process.

2. Line a baking sheet with parchment paper, set the potatoes on the baking sheet and roast in the oven for 25-30 minutes or until a fork can be easily inserted into the potatoes and removed clean.

3. While the potatoes are doing their thing, add 2 tbsp. of butter to a saucepan and bring to medium heat. Add your sliced apples and onions and sauté until they begin to get soft.

4. Add your brown sugar and spices - stir to combine and evenly coat the apples and onions in the spices. The moisture from the onions and apples will marry with the brown sugar and spices to create a sweet n' savory sauce. *Your home should smell amazing at this point.*

5. After the aromas have filled the room, you can add your raisins to the mixture and allow them to simmer for another 10-15 minutes while your sweet potatoes are cooling from roasting. If your mixture looks too dry, feel free to add a few tbsp of water or apple cider.

6. When the potatoes are cool enough to handle, split them in half, and season with salt and pepper to taste (Optional). Add a desired amount of the apple and onion compote to the inside of the warm potato. Garnish with extra raisins and your favorite granola. ***Dig in & enjoy!***

EXTRA TIP: Prep for the week by cutting the casserole into squares and portion it out to have a pre-prepared breakfast for your family throughout the week! Pair with fresh fruit, apple sauce or a smoothie for a well rounded quick start to the day!

Breakfast Croissant Casserole

Serves: 10-12 | Prep Time: 10 minutes | Cook Time 30 minutes

Store bought Croissants (12-20 small; or 8-10 large)

1 lb Breakfast sausage, optional

1 medium onion, diced small

1 Bell pepper, diced small

2 tsp Minced garlic

1 tsp Salt

1/2 tsp Pepper

1 tsp Italian blend seasoning

6 Large eggs

2 cups Milk or Half & half

1 cup Shredded cheese

Optional Add ins:

Mushrooms, Spinach, Bacon, etc.

1. Preheat your oven to 375°F. Cut your croissants into large chunks, and place on a baking sheet to bake for 10 minutes or until golden brown and crispy. This will allow the croissants to crisp up enough to soak up the custard without becoming too soggy as the casserole bakes.

2. In a medium saucepan, brown your breakfast sausage until cooked through, then add your diced onions, bell peppers until cooked thoroughly. *Feel free to play with the ingredients and add your own flare – you know your pantry and fridge.*

3. In a mixing bowl, combine your eggs, milk and seasoning - mix well.

4. To assemble, lightly spray a 9x13 dish or pan with non-stick spray. Toss in your crispy croissant pieces in an even layer.

5. After the meat and veggies have cooled down, evenly distribute over the croissants and toss together to coat the croissants in that sauteed goodness.

6. Then, stream your egg custard over the casserole to make sure the custard touches every nook and cranny of the croissants. Press the ingredients down into the custard to make sure everything is coated - this will ensure the custard will rise evenly while baking.

7. Feel free to add any cheese to the top and prepare to bake.

8. Bake the casserole in a 375°F oven for 35-40 minutes or until the top is golden brown and the custard is set. Allow to cool for 10-15 minutes after removing from the oven and enjoy your *All-In-One Day Starter!*

COMFORT FOOD

"God, grant me the **serenity** to accept the things I cannot change, the courage to change the things I can, and the wisdom to know the difference..."

Excerpt from "Serenity Prayer" Written by Reinhold Neibuhr

Chapter 2

CHOOSE SERENITY

Focus ONLY on what YOU can change

One thing my 'Desert places' taught me is you don't always have control over what happens in life, but you do have control over how you *view it* and how you choose to live *through it!* **Choosing Serenity** in the midst of difficult times isn't easy at all - but the rewards are greater than the sacrifice and you'll be stronger on the other side of your changed perspective.

These **Comfort food** recipes are a physical depiction and reminder to slow down, enjoy the little moments of peace and be thankful for everything you *do* have.

SUB FOR: Sub Andouille for Turkey sausage, Vegan sausage or go meatless if needed. Smoked Turkey parts are amazing in this dish as well.

Cajun Cabbage

Serves: 6-8 | Prep Time: 10 minutes | Cook Time 40 minutes

1 head of Cabbage, thinly sliced & thoroughly washed

1 (12 oz) package of Andouille Sausage, optional

1 Bell Pepper, medium dice

1 medium yellow or red onion, medium dice

2 tsp Minced garlic

1 (28 oz) can Diced tomatoes

1 tbsp Oil (Olive oil, canola, or grapeseed)

1 tsp Salt

1/2 tsp Black pepper

2 tsp Paprika

1 tsp Chili Powder

1/4 tsp Cayenne Pepper

1 tsp Italian seasoning

Welcome to a seat at my family's table. This dish is one of my favorite dishes to eat, paired with some Hot water cornbread and a glass of wine! You can load it up with meat or keep it lean with just the veggies - either way. It won't disappoint.

1. In a large pot, bring your oil up to a medium heat.

2. Sauté sliced sausage until most of the fat has been rendered out. *The smell of andouille should be made into a candle - OMG!*

3. Add your diced onion and bell peppers to the pot and cook until nearly soft. Be sure to scrape any brown bits from the bottom of the pan. Bits = *Added Flavor*

4. Drop your garlic in the flavor pool, stir well, being sure not to let the garlic burn.

5. Throw in all of your seasonings and stir well. *This process is called "blooming" it simply intensifies the flavors of your seasonings.*

6. Add your prepped cabbage to the pot and stir to combine.

7. Once the cabbage has been coated in the goodness of the sausage fat and seasoning, add your canned tomatoes, then stir well.

8. Cover your pot, lower the temperature to a low heat and simmer for 25-30 minutes.

Southern Hot Water Cornbread

Serves: 10-12* | Prep Time: 10 minutes | Cook Time 10 minutes

1 cup All Purpose Flour

1 cup Yellow Cornmeal

1 tsp Baking Powder

2 tsp Salt

1/2 tsp Black pepper

4 tbsp Melted butter

2/3 - 1 cup Boiling water

Canola oil for a shallow fry

Small bowl of water to dip your fingers...I'll explain later.

DISCLAIMER: As this dish is known as a traditional staple in the African American household, many variations exist – this is just mine! It's tastebud approved - Not Grandmother approved.

1. In a mixing bowl, combine your dry ingredients (flour, cornmeal, baking powder, salt, pepper). Stir to combine.

2. Add your melted butter to your dry ingredients to make a sand-like mixture. *Trust the process...It'll come together.*

3. Now slowly stream in your hot water, 1/3 cup at a time, stirring the soon to be golden batter until the dough comes together. As you mix, the dough will form and become one soft mixture. *Be sure not to over mix your dough - over mixing prevents your cornbread from being light and fluffy in the middle with a crisp exterior.*

4. In a large saucepan, bring your oil to a frying temperature of 325-350°F ...or just drop a pinch of your dough in to see if it begins to fry

5. While your oil is rising to temperature, dip your fingertips in the bowl of cold water and pinch off small-medium rounds from the dough to form round or oblong patties then carefully add to the hot oil, laying the dough into the pan away from you, to begin frying.

6. Complete this process until the mixture is all gone. Frying each cornbread round for 2-4 minutes per side until they are golden brown and firm to the touch.

7. Remove them from the pan and place on a wire rack or plate lined with paper towels to dry.

Serving size is dependent upon the size of YOUR portions.

GREAT WITH: Pair this savory companion with your favorite stew, beans or my family's Cajun Cabbage (see Recipe on page 35). You're also welcome to add more butter to the top of these delicious disk after they come right out of the pan.

Kitchen Sweep Goulash

Serves: 8-10 | Prep Time: 10 minutes | Cook Time 10 minutes

1 large White, yellow or red onion

2 Large carrots, peeled and diced

2 Large celery stalks, diced

2 Minced garlic cloves

1 tbsp Tomato paste

1 tbsp Cornstarch to sprinkle over protein

2 lbs. of beef stew meat

1 lb. of elbow noodles

1 large can of crushed tomatoes

4 cups of Stock of choice or water

1. Prepare to cook your goulash stew by dicing all of your aromatics (onion, carrot, celery and garlic) and vegetables of choice into even pieces – *as a shortcut for your aromatics, use a frozen seasoning blend of onions, celery and bell peppers that can be found in the freezer section of your grocery store near the frozen vegetables.*

2. If using a meat protein (Beef stew meat, diced chicken, ground turkey, etc.) season with 1 tsp. of salt and 1/2 tsp. of pepper. Then toss the seasoned meat with 1 tbsp. of cornstarch to help build a shortcut roux (thickening agent made with equal parts flour and fat) during the cooking process.

3. In a stew pot or large skillet set to medium heat, add 2 tbsp. of olive oil to the pan, add your meat to begin searing. The cornstarch will marry with the rendered fat from the meat to make a flavor base for your stew.

4. Once your meat has formed a nice brown crust, remove from the pan, place on a plate to rest while you continue building your stew. (The goal is not to fully cook your protein fully at this stage).

5. Then add in your aromatics (onion, carrot, celery and garlic) and sauté until translucent. Be sure to scrape the brown bits created from the meat off the sides and bottom of the pan- *all of this is added flavor.*

6. When your aromatics have cooked for 2-3 minutes, add in your tomato paste and stir to combine with aromatics.

7. At this point you can add in any additional vegetables you have (squash, mushrooms, eggplant, etc.) and sauté for 2-3 minutes along with your aromatic blend.

8. Here's the time to add your seasoned meat back into the pan to marry their flavors with the vegetables. Stir well.

9. Now add your uncooked elbow noodles, or short noodle of choice, along with 4 cups of stock (chicken stock, beef stock, vegetable broth, etc.).

Optional: Add a boost of flavor by adding a bouquet of fresh herbs to the pot – rosemary, sage and/or thyme would be great.

10. Lower the heat to a simmer, cover the pot and allow to simmer for 40-45 minutes or until your pasta is cooked through and your meat is tender.

11. Allow your stew to cool before serving. And when it's ready, serve it up in a nice bowl paired with crackers, bread or cornbread of choice.

Protein Options (2 lbs)	Starch Options (1 lb)	Vegetable Option (1 lb)	Liquid Option (4 cups)
Beef, Chicken, Beans, Lentils, Chickpeas or whatever is in your kitchen	Potatoes, Rice, Short Pasta, Corn or whatever you have in your kitchen	Mushrooms, Kale, Squash, Chickpeas or...whatever you have in your cupboards	Water, Chicken Stock, Veggie Stock, Beef Broth

TOP U.S. CITIES

with the largest population living in *Food Deserts*.

NO.1 MEMPHIS, TN

> *According to Department of Agriculture data, **32%** of Memphis, Tennessee, residents are low-income and live in areas with insufficient access to groceries.*

NO. 3 RIVERSIDE, CA

NO. 6 NEW ORLEANS, LA

NO. 8 ATLANTA, GA

NO. 10 DALLAS, TX

NO. 11 TAMPA, FL

NO. 14 KANSAS CITY, MO

NO. 16 PHOENIX, AZ

NO. 17 JACKSONVILLE, FL

SOURCE: USAFacts.org - "Which cities have the most people living in food deserts" Published June 2021

DINNER TIME

Chapter 3

DON'T BELIEVE THE MIRAGE

Don't let lies, doubt, negative self-talk and "facts" dictate your outcome.

Nighttime can be prime hours for *worry and anxiety* to run rampant through our minds when dealing with hard times; you start stacking the odds, counting the missing dollars, calculating the missed opportunities and ultimately creating this mirage of failure that really doesn't exist.

However, nighttime also means **Dinner Time** – the space in your day to indulge in something filling and delicious to help create the perfect reward for you conquering another day.

Replace your woes with these great **Dinner Time** recipes that you and your family can enjoy on any night of the week.

*Remember: **Don't believe the mirage!***

This brings back so many memories of my childhood home - late night, tired mom, hyper kids and a hungry family. This dish truly represents the epitome of 'making something out of nothing'. Never underestimate what basic ingredients and a little creativity can do!

Mom's Foil Packet Dinner

Serves: 4-6 | Prep Time: 10 minutes | Cook Time: 45 minutes

1 Medium onion, medium dice

2 Celery stalks, medium dice

2 Carrots, peeled and diced

2 Large potatoes, diced into medium cubes

1 tbsp Olive oil

1.5 tsp Salt, reserve 1/2 tsp

1/2 tsp Black pepper, reserve 1/4 tsp.

1/2 tsp Garlic powder

1 tsp Italian seasoning

2-4 Beef chuck steaks, cubed

2 tbsp Liquid smoke or Worcestershire sauce

1 Small can Crushed tomatoes or V8

1. Cube your steak into medium-large chunks. Season with your reserved salt and pepper and place into a freezer bag. Pour your liquid smoke inside, pull the air out of the freezer bag and secure it tightly. Massage the meat while in the bag until it is completely coated by the liquid smoke. Store and marinate in the fridge overnight.

2. To serve, remove your marinated meat from the fridge and allow it to come to room temperature. Preheat oven to 350°F.

3. In a bowl, take your diced vegetables and pour 1 tbsp. of oil over them, along with your remaining seasonings. Toss to coat evenly.

4. On a baking sheet, arrange 4-6 foil sheets to prepare to fill them with your prepped ingredients. Evenly distribute the seasoned vegetables and potatoes onto each foil sheet, leaving a border around the edge in order to fold the foil into packets.

5. Now you'll begin forming your packets by tucking in the short ends of the packets 2-3 times to ensure no juices escape out the sides during cooking. And leave a window open at the top to stream in your tomato sauce.

6. Peel back the top sides enough to evenly distribute the can of tomatoes between all the foil packets. Then close and tuck the top to secure. Be sure to leave some space in your packets so that steam can circulate properly.

7. Pop your packets into the preheated oven for 35-45 minutes. Remove the baking sheet and allow to cool for 10-15 minutes. Grab a fork and bust that packet open to release the steam. *Now that's some simply good eating!*

Chicken: 3 Ways

Serves: 4 | Prep Time: 10 minutes | Cook Time: 20-30 minutes

4 Boneless Skinless Chicken Breasts or Bone-in Cuts

1 tsp. Salt

1/4 tsp. Pepper

1/2 tsp. Garlic Powder

1/2 tsp. Onion powder

1 tsp. Italian Blend Seasoning

1/2 cup of your choice Salad Dressings (Ranch, French, Italian, etc.)

1 tbsp. of Oil

1/4 cup of Water

1. In a small bowl, add all your seasonings together and mix until combined.
Bonus Add: *Voila! You've just made your own **Seasoning Blend!** This is a great way to control your sodium usage while cooking by making this basic blend in batches and use it throughout the week for breakfast, lunch or dinner.*

2. Prepare your chicken by seasoning both sides liberally with the seasoning blend.

3. In a skillet, bring your oil up to medium high heat and sear both sides of the chicken. 3-4 minutes per side for Boneless cuts; 5-6 minutes per side for Bone-in cuts.

Stove top (preferred for Boneless cuts): After you've seared your chicken on both sides and you've got a great brown crust, pour your dressing of choice right over all of the chicken, being sure to coat each piece evenly. Add your water then lower the heat to a simmer. Cover your skillet and allow it to continue cooking for 15 minutes. The juices from the chicken will combine with the dressing to make an amazingly delicious and easy pan sauce.

Oven (preferred for Bone-in cuts): After you've seared your chicken on both sides and you've achieved that beautiful brown crust, place your chicken pieces into a baking dish lined with foil or parchment paper for easy clean-up. Pour your desired dressing all over your chicken - be sure to evenly coat each piece. Add your water, cover with foil and bake in a 400°F degree oven for 20-25 minutes or until your chicken is cooked through. Remove from the oven and allow to sit for 10-15 minutes. That same pan sauce will continue to create itself during this time.

4. Pair the chicken with your favorite vegetable or starch and you've got dinner in under 45 minutes folks! *Share your chicken creations with me @SurvivingtheFoodDesert*

SIDES TO CONSIDER:

RANCH CHICKEN: Creamy Mashed Potatoes, Mushroom Risotto, Creamed Spinach, Caesar Salad, Brown Rice

FRENCH CHICKEN: Arugula & Spinach Salad, Roasted Cauliflower, Saffron Rice, Grilled Vegetables, Roasted Asparagus

ITALIAN CHICKEN: Roasted Brussels, Charred Broccolini. Roasted Red Potatoes, Garden Salad, Cauliflower Mash

TIP: This is a great dish to portion out throughout the week, pack for lunch or freeze for later.

Stuffed Cornbread

Serves: 6-8 | Prep Time: 30 minutes | Cook Time 25-30 minutes

- 2 boxes Cornbread mix
- 2 cups White or Brown rice, cooked
- 2 tbsp Olive oil
- 2 lbs Ground Beef or Turkey
- 1 Medium onion, diced

- 2 Celery stalks, diced
- 1 Green bell pepper, diced
- 1 bag Frozen mixed vegetables
- 1 tsp Paprika
- 1 tsp Salt
- 1/4 tsp Pepper

- 1/2 tsp Garlic Powder
- 1/2 tsp Cumin
- 1 tsp Chili Powder
- Large can of diced tomatoes

This was indeed a childhood favorite of mine and a staple creation from my mom's bag of low budget tricks. You have your starch, protein, veggies and bread, all in one bite but it allows you to customize it how you like. I've definitely revisited this recipe a few times in my adulthood and it still proves to be a great, economical way to stretch a meal during a busy week.

1. Preheat your oven to 400°F. While your oven is coming to temperature, in a separate bowl, make your boxed cornbread mix according to the box directions and set to the side.

2. In a medium pot, cook 2 cups of rice following the package instructions. **Kitchen Hack:** *Minute rice works perfectly fine - day old rice works great too.*

3. In a skillet set to medium heat, add in olive oil and brown the ground meat until cooked through.

4. Add the diced onion, celery, and bell pepper to the skillet. Sauté until the veggies turn translucent.

5. Add in your seasonings, mixed vegetables and tomatoes. Stir to combine.

6. In a baking dish, arrange a layer of rice on the bottom of your dish. Then top your rice with a layer of the meat and vegetable mixture.

7. Finish the casserole by topping your meat layer by spreading the cornbread batter evenly over the top, being sure the batter touches every corner. *Add shredded cheese to the top if you desire.*

8. Bake for 25-30 minutes or until your cornbread is cooked through and deliciously brown on top.

9. Allow to cool before consuming and cut into squares to serve. Eat as a main dish or along with a salad or additional vegetables.

SWEET TREATS

There is "also glory in our sufferings, because we know that suffering produces perseverance; perseverance, character; and character, hope."

Romans 5:3-4 NIV

TAKE ADVANTAGE OF YOUR RESOURCES

Growth cannot happen where Hope is not present

Christian or not, you have to admit, that statement carries quite a heavy load of truth. I've always said that striving for better and discouragement don't marry well. Striving for better literally means that you possess at least a sliver of *hope*. It's a self-reassuring notion that things will get better, your circumstances can and will change, and there is fruitful and abundant life on the other side of this "Desert". How do I know? Let's just say, I've been in starvation mode more times than I would like-weak, disheartened, parched...yet hopeful.

Ahhh, but when that sweet slice of hope enters your mind, body and soul, sending an electric signal to your spirit that everything is going to be *OK*, your mind opens up, the scales fall from your eyes and new possibilities become apparent and clear. It's time to roll up those sleeves, look around and **use your resources!**

CinnaPeach Cobbler Bake

Serves: 12-15 | Prep Time: 15 minutes | Cook Time: 35-40 minutes

8-large Store-bought cinnamon rolls, cut into small cubes

1 (14 oz.) can Peaches

6 large eggs

2 cups of milk or half and half

1 tsp Vanilla extract

1/4 tsp Ground nutmeg

1 tsp Ground cinnamon

1/4 cup Powdered sugar

Pair with your favorite ice cream and you've got a quick dessert to feed a crowd – or keep to yourself.

1. Preheat your oven to 375ºF.

2. Cut cinnamon rolls into small chunks and layer onto a baking sheet to lightly toast for 8-10 min. *This process allows the bread to absorb the custard without getting super soggy during the baking process.*

3. Once your toasted cinnamon buns have come out of the oven, transfer them into a buttered baking dish or 9x13 pan to begin building your dessert.

4. Drain your canned peaches, reserving your peach syrup separately to make an easy sauce for your cobbler. Cut your drained canned peaches small cubes and evenly distribute them over your cubed cinnamon rolls.

5. In a microwavable bowl or pan on the stove, warm your milk for 2-3 min. Then in a separate bowl, whisk your eggs, extract and spices together until well combined; then slowly stream in your warm milk while whisking at the same time to temper your eggs. *Tempering is the process of gradually bringing your eggs to a warmer temperature without cooking them to prevent scrambling.*

6. Then evenly stream the mixture over your rolls and peaches, being sure to evenly coat the bread. Be sure every corner, nook and cranny is kissed with your custard to ensure even baking.

7. Pop your dish in a preheated 375ºF oven for 35 minutes or until the egg custard is set and the top is golden brown.

8. While you wait, take 1/2 cup of powdered sugar and add 2 tbsp of your reserved peach syrup to make a quick and easy peach sauce to drizzle over your warm cobbler once it's done.

BONUS: Add 1/4 cup of softened cream cheese to make a thicker glaze.

Calas: Creole Rice Fritter

Serves: 12-15 | Prep Time: 15 minutes | Cook Time: 35-40 minutes

2 cups Cooked white rice

2 Eggs

2 tsp Baking Powder

3 tbsp All Purpose Flour

2 tbsp Sugar

1/2 tsp Vanilla extract

Canola Oil, for frying

Powdered Sugar, for dusting

Alternative Toppings:

Cinnamon Sugar or Melted Chocolate

These will be the closest, quickest way to take a trip to New Orleans without all the yeast!

1. In a medium pot, fill your pot 1/3 of the way with canola oil and bring the oil to 325-350 °F to prepare to fry your rice donuts.

2. Follow the package instructions to cook 2 cups of white rice. Place the cooked rice in a mixing bowl and set to the side. *Be sure to rinse the rice before or after cooking to eliminate any extra starch that may cause your rice to become gummy - day old rice works great as well.*

3. In a small bowl, whisk your 2 eggs and add to the bowl of rice.

4. Combine your dry ingredients (flour, baking powder, and sugar) and stir in with the rice and eggs. Mix until well incorporated. Cover the mixture with plastic wrap and refrigerate overnight or until you're ready to begin frying.

5. When you're ready to fry, take 2 spoons or an ice cream scoop, carefully drop a dollop of your donut batter in the oil. Fry your donut balls for 2-3 minutes or until they're golden brown and begin to float to the top.

6. Remove the mini donuts from the oil and place on a paper towel to drain and cool until you finish frying the remainder of your batter.

7. Once they've cooled enough to handle, put a big mound of your donuts on a plate and dust them with powdered sugar to your heart's content.

BONUS: Roll your warm donuts in a cinnamon sugar coating or dip in melted chocolate for a cool spin on this classic. Great with coffee in the morning or a light post dinner dessert.

Boxed Cake Cookies

Serves: 10-12 | Prep Time: 10 minutes | Cook Time 10-12 minutes

Chocolate Chip

1 Box of Yellow Cake Mix

2 Eggs, at room temperature

¼ cup Dark Brown Sugar

½ cup melted Butter

1 cup of Chocolate Chips

Snickerdoodle

1 box of Yellow Cake Mix

2 Eggs, room temperature

¼ cup Light Brown Sugar

½ cup melted Butter

Sugar dust

½ cup Sugar

½ cup Brown Sugar

1 tsp of Cinnamon

Oatmeal Raisin

1 Box of Yellow Cake Mix

2 Eggs, at room temperature

¼ cup Dark Brown Sugar

½ cup melted Butter

1/2 cup of Rolled Oats

¾ cup of Raisins

1 tsp of Vanilla Extract

1 tsp of Ground Cinnamon

½ tsp of Ground Nutmeg

1. Preheat your oven to 350ºF. In a mixing bowl, or standing mixer with the paddle attachment, cream your melted butter and brown sugar together until the sugar has dissolved. Then mix in your eggs and stir to combine.

2. Drop in the store bought cake mix and mix well. *This mixture will be much wetter than a scratch cookie dough, but don't fret! It'll come together.*

3. At this point, you can add in any of your favorite cookie condiments (nuts, raisins, oats, white chocolate, etc.) but chocolate chips will always be my gateway to happiness. Stir and combine well until your cookie fixings are incorporated evenly throughout the batter.

4. Cover your bowl in plastic wrap and refrigerate for 10 minutes to allow the butter to firm up the dough. *This batter can be made a day in advance.*

5. Remove your chilled dough, use a spoon or ice cream scoop to scoop out your cookie dough and place on a baking sheet lined with parchment paper.

6. Bake in a preheated oven set to 350ºF degrees for 10-12 minutes or until your cookies are as *ooey gooey* or crunchy as you desire.

Chapter 5

THINK OUTSIDE OF THE BOX

Get Creative – Make Something out of Nothing

While I'm sure we've all found ourselves in a place of drought, of desperation, thrusting us into survival mode - the only true option you have is to persevere because we dare not give up and forfeit the opportunity to see what's on the other side of our newfound strength birthed out a place in your soul you didn't even know existed.

The choice to triumph and persevere takes sheer creativity, thinking outside of the box...and sometimes, simply making something out of nothing! Find joy within your desert place and try one or all of these **Fun Foods** to lift your spirits.

Fried CauliNuggets

Serves: 6-8 | Prep Time: 8-10 minutes | Cook Time: 15 minutes

1 head of Cauliflower - broken down into bite size florets

3 cups Panko or Italian bread crumbs, (seasoned with 1 tsp of Italian seasoning, 1/2 tsp garlic powder, 1 tsp of chili powder)

Canola Oil for frying

Yogurt Coating

3 tbsp Milk

1 tsp Salt

2 tbsp Grainy mustard

1 tbsp Worcestershire sauce

Due to my own health struggles and battles with food sensitivities, I was forced to adopt a veggie forward diet, mainly vegan-pescatarian - but I missed all the fried goodness I used to eat with no guilt. This is one of my favorite "cheat" meals that cures my fried food cravings!

1. Prepare a pot or deep skillet with your frying oil, bringing it to a temperature of 325-350°F.

2. Take your cauliflower florets and coat them evenly in your yogurt coating - be sure to shake off the excess to prevent your batter from clumping. *Using a fork will make this process easier.*

3. Then take your yogurt covered nuggets and toss them in your breadcrumbs to coat - place on a wire rack until your oil is ready to use.

4. Repeat the dredge process until you've coated all your nuggets. *You can also freeze or refrigerate your nuggets at this step if you'd like to fry them at a later time.*

5. Once your oil comes to temperature, carefully pop your nuggets into the oil and allow them to fry for 2-3 minutes.

6. As your cauliflower gets golden brown and floats to the top, remove them from the oil and place them on a paper towel to soak up any extra oil. Repeat this process until all of your nuggets are golden brown and crispy.

7. Allow your nuggets to cool and pair them with your homemade remoulade for a great snack or faux fried "fish" nugget dinner minus the guilt.

Remoulade Dipping Sauce:

1 cup of Mayo
2 tbsp of Mustard
3 dashes of Hot sauce, or more if you like
2 tsp of Creole Seasoning
1 tbsp of Pickle juice and/or finely
    chopped pickles or dill relish
2 tsp of Worcestershire sauce
Juice of half a Lemon
Fresh herbs, optional

Combine all ingredients together.

Fruit Cocktail Dump Cobbler

Serves: 16-20 | Prep Time: 8-10 minutes | Cook Time: 40-45 minutes

2 large cans (or 4 Medium cans) of Fruit Cocktail

1 box of White or Yellow Cake Mix

1/2 cup of melted Butter

Optional: Add store bought granola to the top for a crunchy topping

Great sweet treat for family night, office party or the holidays.

1. Preheat your oven to 350°F.

2. Pour your cans of fruit cocktail into a buttered 9x13 baking dish.

2. Evenly distribute the cake mix on top of the fruit cocktail.

4. Lightly stir your cake mix into the fruit to form your "cake" batter. *If a little white shows from the cake mix, it's totally fine, it'll soak in with the syrup from the fruit cocktail or turn into a crispy topping while baking*

5. Drizzle your melted 1/2 stick of butter all over the top of the cobbler then bake for 40-45 minutes or until the cake mix is golden brown and the cake mix is cooked through.

6. Remove your dish from the oven and allow to cool for 10-15 minutes.

7. Spoon your cobbler out and top with your favorite ice cream - *vanilla bean would be great!*

Munchie Bars

Serves: 10-12 | Prep Time: 90 minutes | Cook Time: 20 minutes

1 cup (2 sticks) Unsalted butter, at room temperature

1/2 cup Sugar

2 cups All Purpose flour

1/8 tsp Salt

Peanut Butter frosting

1 cup Peanut Butter

2 cups Powdered sugar

1/2 cup Milk

Ganache Base

2 cups Chocolate chips or bars, melted

½ cup Heavy cream or Half and Half

1. Preheat your oven to 350ºF. Prepare your shortbread dough in a standing mixer or bowl by combining your butter, sugar, flour and salt until it forms a loose dough.

2. Line a baking dish with parchment paper and press the dough into the bottom of the dish to form your crust. *It'll look like the dough won't stretch, but I promise, it will.*

3. After your dough has been evenly pressed, take a fork and poke holes all over the dough to let air escape during baking. Bake the crust in a 350ºF degrees oven for 8-10 minutes.

4. While your crust is baking, prepare your peanut butter filling and chocolate ganache and set to the side. Gather your toppings and get ready to go wild on this delicious blank canvas.

6. Once your crust has baked, remove it from the oven and allow it to cool for 10-15 minutes. Spread your peanut butter frosting over the top in an even layer. Place into the fridge for 10 minutes to set.

7. After the frosting has firmed up a bit, take your melted chocolate ganache and pour over the peanut butter layer to create a layer of chocolate - use an offset spatula, spoon or knife to smooth out the ganache so it creates an even layer.

8. Now take your desired toppings and sprinkle all over the top .

9. Place your munchie bar into the freezer to set for 2 hours or overnight.

10. Remove from the freezer, run a knife around the edge of the dish to loosen the dough and chocolate from the sides and pull the entire bar out from the dish using the parchment paper.

TOPPING SUGGESTIONS:
Pretzels, chips, cereal, white chocolate drizzle, sea salt, chocolate candies, etc. – *let your imagination fly!*

Food Desert
RESOURCE GUIDE

Go – Learn – Donate – Volunteer!

Whether you're a survivor of the **food** desert, still looking for nourishment or blessed to feast off an abundance - we all need to know the great seeds that are being planted around us helping to ensure we **live & eat well!**

Take a look through these national & local initiatives, nonprofits, community gardens and more, helping to close the food equity gap in our communities.

Help *cultivate our communities* by joining forces with one of these great organizations so we can **all**, one day, live in *delicious harmony!*

ALABAMA
Eat South
Montgomery
eatsouth.org

Magic City Harvest
Birmingham
magiccityharvest.org

ALASKA
Beans Café
Anchorage
beanscafe.org

Food Bank of Alaska
foodbankofalaska.org

ARIZONA
Farm Express
Phoenix
www.activatefoodaz.org/farmexpress

ARKANSAS
Arkansas Hunger Relief Alliance
arhungeralliance.org

CALIFORNIA
Healthy Retail SF
San Francisco
healthyretailsf.org

Seeds of Hope
Los Angeles
seedsofhopela.org

(LAFPC) Los Angeles Food Policy Council
Los Angeles
goodfoodla.org

LA Compost
LA County
lacompost.org

SUPRMARKT
Los Angeles
suprmarkt.la

FEAST
Los Angeles
feastforall.org

Food Finders
Lakewood
foodfinders.org

Garden School Foundation
Los Angeles
gardenschoolfoundation.org

COLORADO
GrowHaus
thegrowhaus.org

Huerta Urbana
focuspoints.org/huerta-urbana

Denver Food Rescue
Denver
denverfoodrescue.org

DELAWARE
Sunday Breakfast Mission
Wilmington
sundaybreakfastmission.org

Food Bank of Delaware
fbd.org

The Urban Garden Initiative (TUGI)
theurbangardeninitiative.org

Delaware Center of Horticulture
thedch.org

FLORIDA
Food For Thought Outreach
fftfl.org

IDAHO
Shared Harvest Community Garden
Coeur d'Alene
sharedharvestgarden.org

The Hunger Coalition
Bellevue
thehungercoalition.org

ILLINOIS
Dion's Chicago Dream
Chicago
dionschicagodream.com

Growing Home Inc
Chicago
www.growinghomeinc.org

Dekalb Community Gardens
Dekalb County
www.dekalbgardens.org

Chicago Food Policy Action Council
chicagofoodpolicy.com

Feed My Starving Children (FMSC)
fmsc.org

Impact Culinary
impactculinary.org

INDIANA
Soul Food Project
Indianapolis
soulfoodprojectindy.org

Flanner House
Indianapolis
flannerhouse.org

IOWA
Tapestry Farms
Davenport
tapestryfarms.org

KANSAS
Common Ground Community Garden
Lawrence
lawrenceks.org/common-ground

The MERC CO-OP
Lawrence
www.themerc.coop

GEORGIA
The Grocery Spot
Atlanta
thegroceryspot.org

C.H.O.I.C.E.S.
choicesforkids.org

Golden Harvest Food Bank
Augusta
goldenharvest.org

Augusta Locally Grown
Augusta
www.augustalocallygrown.org

MASSACHUSETTS
Daily Table
Boston
www.dailytable.org

Mill City Grows
Lowell
www.millcitygrows.org

MICHIGAN
Detroit People's Food Co-op
Detroit
dbcfsn.org/detroit-people-s-food-co-op

Detroit Hives
Detroit
detroithives.org

MINNESOTA
The Open Door, Garden to Table
Eagan
theopendoorpantry.org/garden-to-table-program

Appetite for Change
Minneapolis
appetiteforchangemn.org

Urban Farms MN
urbanrootsmn.org

MISSOURI
MARSH Food Cooperative
St. Louis
marshlifeart.wordpress.com

The Giving Grove
Kansas City
www.givinggrove.org

Cultivate KC
Kansas City
www.cultivatekc.org

NEBRASKA
Community Crops
Lincoln
communitycrops.org

No More Empty Pots Food Hub
Omaha
nmepomaha.org

The BIG Garden
Omaha
biggarden.org

Big Muddy Urban Farm
Omaha
bigmuddyurbanfarm.org

NEVADA
Garden Farms of Nevada
Las Vegas
gardenfarms.net

NEW HAMPSHIRE
Hillsborough Community Gardens
snhs.org/services/community-gardens

Stark Farm Community Garden
Manchester
starkfarmcommunitygarden.com

New Hampshire Food Bank
nhfoodbank.org

NEW JERSEY
C.R.O.P.S. NJ
cropsnj.org

NEW MEXICO
MoGro
mogro.net

NEW YORK
Rethink Food
New York
rethinkfood.org

Corbin Hill Food Project
Harlem
corbinhill-foodproject.org

City Harvest
New York
cityharvest.org

Eagle Street Rooftop Farm
Brooklyn
rooftopfarms.org

Edible Schoolyard NYC
New York
edibleschoolyardnyc.org

Contoe Family Life Center
Conetoe
conetoelife.org

Oasis Fresh Market
Tulsa
oasisfreshmarkets.net

Freestore Food Bank
freestorefoodbank.org

Black Food Sovereignty Coalition
Portland
blackfoodnw.org

Alberta Co-op
Portland
alberta.coop

Neighborhood House Food Pantry
Portland
nhpdx.org/food-security

Central Oregon Locavore
Central Oregon
centraloregonlocavore.org

Outgrowing Hunger
Portland
outgrowinghunger.org

412 Rescue
Pittsburgh
412foodrescue.org

4dwn Project
Dallas
4dwn.org

Bonton Farms
Dallas
bontonfarms.org

Café Momentum
Dallas
cafemomentum.org

City Square
Dallas
www.citysquare.org

Crossroads Community Services
Dallas
ccsdallas.org

Fresh Houwse Grocery
Houston
blackfarmerbox.com/fresh-houwse-grocery

For Oak Cliff
Oak Cliff/Dallas
www.foroakcliff.org

Funky Town Fridge
Ft. Worth
funkytownfridge.org

Harmony Community Dev. Corp
Dallas
www.harmonycdc.org

Hunger Busters
Dallas
hungerbusters.org

Jacob's Harvest
Dallas
jacobsharvest.org

Jubilee Food Market
Waco
missionwaco.org/our-programs/social-enterprise/jubilee-food-market

La Bajada Urban Youth Farm Park
Trinity Groves
mp0664.wixsite.com/urbanyouthfarm

MLK Recreation Center
Dallas
dallasmlkcenter.com

Minnie's Food Pantry
Plano
minniesfoodpantry.org

North Texas Food Bank
Dallas
ntfb.org

Oak Cliff Veggie Project
Dallas
oakcliffveggieproject.org

Restorative Farms
Dallas/Hatcher
restorativefarms.org

Pan African Connection
Oak Cliff
panafricanconnection.com

Profound Food/Microfarms
Lucas
profoundmicrofarms.com

Roots Food Group
Dallas

Southpoint Community Market
South Dallas
facebook.com/
SouthpointCommunityMarket

Sunny South Dallas Food Park
South Dallas
fairparkdallas.com
Search: Sunny South

Dallas Food Park
West Dallas Cultural Center
West Dallas
dallascityhall.com
Search: West Dallas Cultural Center

TENNESSEE
Nashville Food Project
Nashville
thenashvillefoodproject.org

WASHINGTON D.C.
Wangari Gardens
wangarigardens.wordpress.com

Good Food Markets
Washington
goodfoodmarkets.com

Twin Oaks Community
Gardensites.google.com/site/
twinoaksdc

DC Food Project
Washington
dcfoodproject.org

DC Hunger Solutions
dchunger.org

WYOMING
Wyoming Food For Thought Project
wyomingfood forthoughtproject.org/

VIRGINIA
Feeding Southwest Virginia
feedingswva.org

Northern Virginia Food Rescue
nova-fr.org

UTAH
Open Doors Utah
opendoorsutah.org

NATIONWIDE
Academy of Culinary Nutrition
culinarynutrition.com

All of Us Research
allofus.nih.gov

A Well Fed World (AWFW)
awellfedworld.org

DiaTribe Foundation (Diabetes Education)
diatribe.org/foundation

PLEZI *Co-owned by former first lady, Michelle Obama*
plezi.com

Balcony Box
balcony-box.com

Fair Food Network
fairfoodnetwork.org

Fresh Food Connect
freshfoodconnect.org

Food Empowerment Project
foodispower.org

Food Recovery Network
foodrecoverynetwork.org

Food Tank
foodtank.com

Imperfect Foods
imperfectfoods.com

Move for Hunger
moveforhunger.org

Sea Share
seashare.org

American Heart Association
heart.org

Guide does not include organizations from all states in the U.S.A. This is a starting point to encourage further exploration into the great work that's already being done in your neck of the woods.

Communities can
survive with
Access alone

However...

In order to THRIVE,
there must be

Access + Education

Printed in the USA
CPSIA information can be obtained
at www.ICGtesting.com
LVRC080940260124
769968LV00014B/297